Don't Be a "Waster of Sorrows"

Don't Be a "Waster of Sorrows"

Nine Ways Our Sorrows Can Lead
to a Deeper Spiritual Life

Peter C. Wilcox, STD

WIPF & STOCK · Eugene, Oregon

DON'T BE A "WASTER OF SORROWS"
Nine Ways our Sorrows Can Lead to a Deeper Spiritual Life

Wipf & Stock
An Imprint of Wipf and Stock Publishers
199 W. 8th Ave., Suite 3
Eugene, OR 97401

www.wipfandstock.com

ISBN 13: 978-1-4982-0733-1

Manufactured in the U.S.A.   03/23/2015

To my mother and father, who found it difficult to talk about their sorrows in life. Also, to all my clients through the years, for their strength and courage in sharing their sorrows with me, which has enabled me to face my own. May we all find peace.

Contents

Introduction

THE WELL-KNOWN AUSTRIAN LYRIC poet and noted spiritual writer Rainer Maria Rilke wrote a collection of ten reflective poems between 1912 and 1922, entitled *Duino Elegies*. They are intensely religious, mystical poems that weigh beauty and existential suffering. At one point in this poem, he encourages the reader not to be a "waster of sorrows." Then, in his more popular work, *Letters to a Young Poet*, Rilke encourages his young friend to use his sorrows in a positive way as a means to help him grow in holiness.

And isn't this the challenge for all of us? It is not a gentle world. Everyone has sorrows in life of one kind or another. The important question is not whether we have sorrows or not, but what can we do with them so that we don't waste them? The reality is that what we do with our sorrows can have a tremendous impact on our growth as a person, psychologically, emotionally, and spiritually.

In over thirty years as a psychotherapist, I have listened to people's stories about their lives. Often, a part of their stories involve sorrows of one kind or another. How people handle them has truly been inspiring and in some cases amazing to me. A friend told me once that if we don't struggle to integrate our sorrows into our lives in a healthy way, they will come back to haunt us. As I listened to my clients over the years, I have often wondered why some people become overwhelmed by their sorrows and seem to buckle beneath them while others learn to integrate them into their lives in a way that leads to growth. For each of us, the real question and challenge is: How do we do this? How do we use our suffering and sorrows in life to help us grow in a positive way so that we don't end up wasting them?

Reflecting on his own struggles in life, Martin Luther King Jr. said, "Recognizing the necessity for suffering I have tried to make of it a virtue. If only to save myself from bitterness, I have attempted to see my personal ordeals as an opportunity to transform myself and heal the people involved in the tragic situation. I have lived these last few years with the conviction that unearned suffering is redemptive."[1]

In addition to our own personal sorrows, there is also the reality of the pain and sorrows of others—sometimes not just this or that person, but the sorrows of entire countries and nations. How do we respond to their sorrows? In a realistic way, is there anything we can do to help alleviate the pain of others? Rather than becoming numb to the immense suffering of others, how can we strive to be a true brother or sister to them? And, given the reality that suffering or sorrow is one of the universal conditions of being alive, how can we share our mutual vulnerability so that we can connect with others in their sorrows rather than feel separated from them?

This book is an invitation to discover how we can learn to integrate our sorrows into our own lives so that we can grow psychologically and spiritually. It suggests nine ways that we can reflect on our sorrows to deepen our spiritual lives, so that, as Rilke wrote to his young friend, we don't "waste them."

1. King, "Suffering and Faith," 41.

1

It Is Not a Gentle World

IN THE MUSICAL LES *Misérables*, Fantine, a poor young woman who is forced by circumstances to become a prostitute, sings a beautiful song entitled, "I Dreamed a Dream." It speaks of her sorrows in life.

> There was a time when love was blind
> And the world was a song
> And the song was exciting
> There was a time
> Then it all went wrong
>
> I dreamed a dream in time gone by
> When hope was high
> And life worth living
> I dreamed that love would never die
> I dreamed that God would be forgiving
> Then I was young and unafraid
> And dreams were made and used and wasted . . .
>
> But there are dreams that cannot be
> And there are storms we cannot weather

> I had a dream my life would be
> So different from this hell I'm living
> So different now from what it seemed
> Now life has killed the dream I dreamed[1]

It is not a gentle world. Everyone goes through difficulties in life of one kind or another. Everyone has sorrows that they struggle with, personally, professionally, and communally. And, like Fantine, everyone struggles at times not to let our dreams die—dreams about ourselves, dreams about some part of our life, dreams about some dimension of our world. We don't want life to "kill the dreams I dreamed."

In his *Duino Elegies*, Rainer Maria Rilke encouraged people who were going through difficulties not to be what he called a "waster of sorrows."[2] Isn't this the challenge for each of us? Rilke knew that the sorrows we experience in life can do many things to us, and he wanted people not to "waste them" but to use them in a positive way. But how do we do this? How do we prevent our sorrows in life from "killing our dreams" and allow them to bring us new life?

Jesus and His Sorrows

Jesus certainly experienced sorrows in his life. In fact, there are at least two times in the New Testament when Jesus cried. We know that he cried when his good friend Lazarus died. In chapter 11 of John's Gospel, we read that when Jesus learned that Lazarus had died, he went to his home.

> Mary went to Jesus, and as soon as she saw him she threw herself at his feet, saying, "Lord, if you had been here, my brother would not have died." At the sight of her tears, and those of the Jews who followed her, Jesus

1. This musical is based on the French historical novel by Victor Hugo, first published in 1862. It is generally considered one of the greatest novels of the nineteenth century.

2. Rilke, *Duino Elegies*, 79.

said in great distress, with a sigh that came straight from the heart, "Where have you put him?" They said, "Lord, come and see." Jesus wept; and the Jews said, "See how much he loved him!" (John 11:32–36)

Jesus allowed himself to cry over the loss of a good friend.

Jesus also experienced great sorrow in his agony in the garden of Gethsemane. Luke says in his Gospel that Jesus prayed there "in his anguish . . . even more earnestly, and his sweat fell to the ground like great drops of blood" (Luke 22:44). All of us experience personal sorrows in life and sometimes we have to struggle not to allow those sorrows to cause something inside of us to die. Our sorrow might be the death of a family member or friend. It might be the failure of a relationship or the loss of a job. For others, it might be fighting an addiction or struggling with a physical, mental, or emotional problem. No matter what the source of our sorrow, we certainly don't want to "waste it."

There are other kinds of sorrows that we can also experience that are larger than our own personal sorrows. These are rooted in communities, in societies, in countries, in the human condition. Sometimes they are so overwhelming that they are difficult to fathom. How do we understand the immense suffering of people in our cities and other countries? And yet, these kinds of problems also created great sorrow in Jesus and caused him to cry. In Luke's Gospel, we read that Jesus actually wept over the immense suffering in the city of Jerusalem. "As he drew near and came in sight of the city he shed tears over it and said, "If you in your turn had only understood on this day the message of peace! But, alas, it is hidden from your eyes!" (19:41–42).

How can we fathom this kind of suffering? How do we react when we learn about the poverty of nations, of children not having enough to eat, of hurricanes and tornadoes killing thousands of people and destroying entire parts of countries? Back in the 1980s, there was a musical entitled *The Human Comedy*. It was the story of a teenager who was growing up in poverty in an inner city with crime all around him. He just couldn't understand why life had to be so difficult. Why did people have to struggle so much? Why

3

was there so much suffering and sorrow and violence all around him? As he pondered these questions, he got on a bus and rode all night around the city, crying. His mother was panicking because he hadn't come home. Finally, in the morning, he came back home and began talking to his mother about all of this. After patiently listening to his questions, she told him:

> It was pity that made you cry. . . . Pity, not for this person or that person who is suffering, but for all things—for the very nature of things. Unless a man has pity he is inhuman and not yet truly a man, for out of pity comes a bond which heals. Only good men weep. . . . There will always be pain in things. . . . Knowing this does not mean that a man shall despair. The good man will seek to take pain out of things. The foolish man will not even notice it except in himself. And the evil man will drive pain deeper into things and spread it about wherever he goes.[3]

There is a great sadness in life when we ponder the immense tragedies that occur in the lives of other people on a daily basis. They appear to be so overwhelming that they can almost make us numb. Often, we are afraid to stay with these thoughts, wondering how these situations are ever going to change and become better. What can we do? How can we help? How can we seek "to take the pain out of things"? How can we allow these realities not to kill our dreams about life? Can we do anything not to become a "waster of sorrows"? For the past several years, I have been volunteering at the Franciscan Center in downtown Baltimore. It is located in a very poor section of the city and we serve the very poor, young and old; the homeless; drug addicts; alcoholics; people with many physical, mental, and emotional issues; the disenfranchised; many races and nationalities; single people and families, in a variety of ways. We feed a hot meal to over 400 people five days a week, distribute clothing, help in emergency financial situations, teach people how to write resumes and apply for jobs, and help people find shelter. Generally, I help with serving food to people. As I spend

---

3. Smith and Pryce, *Reading for Power*, 171, quoting from the book by William Saroyan on which the musical was based.

my day there, I often wonder about the stories of these people. What are their lives like? What has made their lives so difficult? Is there a way out of this kind of daily routine for them? Over the years, I have gotten to know several of them. In my conversations with them, I have discovered people who have often struggled with many hardships but who also have found ways of coping with their difficulties in some very constructive ways. They too have not wanted to be a "waster of sorrows." So, what is the difference? Why do some people become crushed under their sorrows and others use them in a positive way for growth? Together, let's look at some ways that our sorrows can help us grow in holiness.

2

The Importance of Grieving Our Sorrows

PERHAPS ONE OF THE most challenging dimensions of our spiritual and psychological lives is to try and find ways to not "waste our sorrows." But how can we do this? How do we deal with our sorrows so that nothing inside of us dies? How can we discover something positive, something life-giving in our sorrows, so that our dreams don't die?

The first thing we need to do is to grieve our sorrows. Every great loss demands that we choose life again. And in order to do this, we need to grieve our sorrows. If we don't do this, the pain we have not grieved will always stand between us and growing in life. When we don't grieve our sorrows, a part of us becomes caught in the past and eventually will find a way to negatively influence our lives.

Grieving is not about forgetting. Rather, grieving allows us to heal and to remember with love rather than pain. It requires a sorting out process. One by one, you try to let go of the things that are gone and mourn for them. One by one, you take hold of the things that have become a part of who you are and gradually begin to build again. This is not to suggest that this process of grieving is easy, only that it is necessary.

In Mitch Albom's book *Tuesdays with Morrie*, Morrie Schwartz is interviewed by TV personality Ted Koppel. Morrie was dying from Lou Gehrig's disease (amyotrophic lateral sclerosis). Ted asked Morrie how he coped with facing the end of his life.

> "Ted," he said, "when all this started, I asked myself, 'Am I going to withdraw from the world, like most people do, or am I going to live?' I decided I'm going to live—or at least try to live—the way I want, with dignity, with courage, with humor, with composure.
>
> "There are some mornings when I cry and cry and mourn for myself. Some mornings, I am so angry and bitter. But it doesn't last too long. Then I get up and say, 'I want to live . . .' "So far, I've been able to do it. Will I be able to continue? I don't know. But I'm betting on myself that I will."[1]

Interestingly enough, as we mourn our sorrows, it can even be helpful and healing to feel sorry for ourselves at times. It helps us cope with all of the emotions we are experiencing. But many people feel that this is a weakness—that we shouldn't let ourselves feel sorry for ourselves. Again, in *Tuesdays with Morrie*, the author, Mitch Albom, asked Morrie if he ever felt sorry for himself.

> "Sometimes, in the mornings," he said. "That's when I mourn. I feel around my body, I mourn my fingers and my hands—whatever I can still move—and I mourn the slow, insidious way in which I'm dying. But then I stop mourning."
>
> Just like that? "I give myself a good cry if I need it. But then I concentrate on all the good things still in my life. On the people who are coming to see me. On the stories I'm going to hear. On you—if it's Tuesday. Because we're Tuesday people."
>
> I grinned. Tuesday people.
>
> "Mitch, I don't allow myself any more self-pity than that. A little each morning, a few tears, and that's all."[2]

---

1. Albom, *Tuesdays with Morrie*, 21–22.
2. Ibid., 56–57.

Morrie understood the value of mourning for himself at times and then trying to make the most of his day.

Part of the grieving process involves acceptance, which is never easy. That is why it's a process—trying to accept the reality that is causing our sorrow. When our first child, a son, was stillborn, our sorrow felt overwhelming. The pain and anguish of losing him seemed insurmountable. Gradually, with the help of others, our sorrow began to diminish. Then, in order not to be "a waster of sorrows," my wife and I became involved in the organization called Compassionate Friends, where we tried to help others who had lost a child. In addition, grief counseling became one of the major focus points in my counseling career for over thirty years. Moreover, through the years I have given numerous conferences to this group as a way of saying, "Thank you."

So much in life depends on how we see things—the attitude that we have. Marcel Proust said that the voyage of discovery lies not in seeking new vistas but in having new eyes. There is an old Carolina story I like about a country boy who had a great talent for carving beautiful dogs out of wood. Every day he sat on his porch whittling, letting the shavings fall around him. One day a visitor, greatly impressed, asked him the secret of his art. "I just take a block of wood and whittle off the parts that don't look like a dog," he replied. Accepting things in life can be like this. It depends on how we see something. If we see something in a certain way, we can become stuck in our sorrows. But if we struggle to see something in a different way, it can gradually lead to new life. As Morrie struggled to accept his situation, he told Koppel about a friend of his, Maurice Stein, who had taught with Morrie at Brandeis University and was going deaf. "Koppel imagined the two men together one day, one unable to speak, the other unable to hear. What would that be like? 'We will hold hands,' Morrie said. 'And there'll be a lot of love passing between us. Ted, we've had thirty-five years of friendship. You don't need speech or hearing to feel that.'"[3] Attitude is everything. And, it leads to acceptance.

3. Ibid., 70–71.

Reflecting on the importance of our attitudes, pastor and spiritual writer Charles Swindoll said,

> The longer I live, the more I realize the impact of attitude in life. Attitude, to me, is more important than facts. It is more important than the past, than education, than money, than circumstances, than failures, than successes, than what other people think or say or do. It is more important than appearance, giftedness, or skill. It will make or break a company, a church, a home. The remarkable thing is we have a choice every day regarding the attitude we will embrace for that day. We cannot change our past. We cannot change the fact that people will act in a certain way. We cannot change the inevitable. The only thing we do is play on the one string we have, and that is our attitude. I am convinced that life is 10 percent what happens to me and 90 percent how I react to it. And so it is with you. We are in charge of our attitudes.[4]

Even Martin Luther King Jr. struggled to accept his own personal sorrows. At one point he said: "My personal trials have also taught me the value of unmerited suffering. As my sufferings mounted I soon realized that there were two ways in which I could respond to my situation: either to react with bitterness or seek to transform the suffering into a creative force. I decided to follow the latter course."[5]

In our everyday lives, we all experience sorrow. If we simply try to spiritualize them away or dismiss or run away from them, we cannot use them to grow. If, as Ram Dass suggests, life is the ultimate spiritual teacher, we cannot learn unless we attend school. This usually means allowing ourselves not only to be touched by life, but to fully participate in it. We learn by experience. The unexperienced life does not teach anybody anything. There are no spiritual shortcuts.

Maybe the most important thing to understand about the many strategies we use to shelter ourselves from grieving our

---

4. Quoted from Zuck, *Speaker's Quote Book*, 28.
5. King, "Suffering and Faith," 41.

sorrows is that none of them lead to healing. Although denial, rationalization, substitution, and avoidance may numb the pain of our loss, every one of them hurts us in some far more fundamental ways. None is respectful toward life or toward process. None acknowledges our inner capacity for finding meaning or wisdom. Grieving is the way we can heal from our sorrows. There are no shortcuts in this process if we want to use our sorrows in a positive way and not waste them. We cannot protect ourselves from sorrow. Yet, many people still do not know how to grieve and heal their sorrows. This makes it difficult to find the courage to participate fully in life. At some deep level, it may make us unwilling to be open or present to others, or we might find it difficult to become attached or intimate. Many people have become emotional couch potatoes because they have not allowed themselves to grieve and find healing.

Unless we learn to grieve, we will need to protect ourselves from pain. In addition, we may not be able to risk having anything that really matters to us or allow ourselves to be touched or to truly care for someone or be cared about. Untouched, we will suffer anyway but we will not be transformed by our suffering. Grieving may be one of the most important and fundamental life skills. It is the way that the heart can heal from loss and go on to love again and grow wise.

3

The Importance of Praying
Our Sorrows

WHEN I WAS A child growing up in West Virginia, the Catholic sisters always told us to "offer up" our sorrows to Jesus. They said this was important because in this way we could unite our sufferings with the sufferings of Jesus on the cross and become one with him. Moreover, they said we could even make this a very special prayer and "offer it up" for someone else—either a soul in purgatory or a living person. They taught us that this could be a very special way of praying.

We don't hear very much any more about this traditional teaching of our faith, and yet today it is still very important to understand because it continues to mean a great deal to many people. From a classical theological perspective, we believe that because we are the body of Christ, the church, we can affect one another in a variety of ways. Not only can I participate in the death and resurrection of Jesus, the Paschal Mystery, by uniting my suffering, my crosses, my sorrows to his, but I can also make my suffering a special prayer that I offer for others. This, then, from a traditional theological perspective, is the way we know that our crosses and sorrows in life have meaning. If we can do this, we will not be a "waster of sorrow" but will use our sorrow to help others.

From a more contemporary perspective, Henri Nouwen believed that one of the more insidious ideas around in recent years has tried to make us think of prayer primarily as an activity of the mind that involves above all our intellectual capacities. This prejudice reduces prayer to speaking with God or thinking about God. Prayer isn't strictly a mental activity any more than it is strictly an emotional activity. It is an experience of our *whole* being.

But how can we pray when our heart is full of sorrow? Is there a way to pray that isn't found on the regular prayer menu? Is there a way to pray that has little to do with petition and intercession and getting God to fix things? David Steindl-Rast says that anything we do with our whole heart can be a prayer. T. S. Eliot wrote about a "deep center" within each of us that he called "the still point." "Except for the point, the still point, there would be no dance," he wrote.[1] Everyone possesses this center, this still point. It is the quiet core where God's Spirit dwells in us, and this can give us a different way of praying in our sorrow. "Do you not know that . . . God's Spirit dwells in you?" (1 Cor 3:16, NRSV). Sometimes we tend to forget this. Yet in some holy place within us, God lives and moves and has being (2 Cor 6:16). At this inmost center of our being, a place where we are deeply and profoundly known and loved by God, we can pray our sorrows. It is here that we attach ourselves to God. But this is also where God attaches himself to us. Ultimately, as Hildegard of Bingen said, the still point is a love meeting, an embrace. She wrote, "God hugs you. You are encircled by the arms of the mystery of God."[2] God's hug—what a wonderful image! In our sorrows, maybe all we need is to allow ourselves to be hugged.

Author and Presbyterian minister Eugene Peterson was quoted in an interview as saying, "the assumption of spirituality is that God is always doing something before I know it. So the task is not to get God to do something I think needs to be done, but to become aware of what God is doing so that I can respond to it and participate and take delight in it."[3] This is the motivation behind

1. Eliot, "Burnt Norton."
2. Uhlein, *Meditations with Hildegard of Bingen*, 90.
3. Clapp, "Eugene Peterson," 25.

this kind of prayer. We try to find quiet times, places of stillness, that allow the Lord, who is already within us, to love us. In our times of sorrow, we can just sit with the Lord and allow him to hug us.

However, this idea of just sitting in the God's presence can be more difficult than we think. We are not used to "just sitting" with God. In fact, in our fast-paced world, we are not used to sitting for anything for very long. And we certainly are not used to praying this way. And yet, this can be so helpful in terms of praying our sorrows. The story is told about an old peasant and St. John Vianney, the Curé d'Ars. It seems as though this old gentleman would simply come into an empty church and just sit for hours. One day, the Cure d'Ars decided to ask him what he did during all these hours in church. The old peasant replied, "Nothing. I just look at him and he looks at me." This old peasant understood what sitting in God's presence and allowing him to love us was all about.

It is interesting to recall that even on the last night of Jesus' life, when he was filled with sorrow, he invited his disciples to sit while he prayed. "And they went to a place which was called Gethsemani; and He said to His disciples, "Sit here while I pray" (Mark 14:32, NRSV).

It was the eve of Jesus' death. He was on the verge of being arrested. The hour was late, and the crisis surrounding the disciples had been very draining on all of them. Jesus took them to a garden to wait through the long night. Did he ask them to pray? To plead his case? No. "Sit down here and rest," he said. "I'll pray." "Sit here while I pray." Could this be an invitation not only to his disciples but to us as well? Does he want us to sit and rest while he prays? Could it be that this type of prayer requires no particular words but only that we be still so that he can pray within us? Saint Paul wrote, ". . . the Spirit helps us in our weakness; for we do not know how to pray as we ought, but that very Spirit intercedes with sighs too deep for words" (Rom 8:26, NRSV). The Spirit *does* pray in us while we rest. He prays with sighs too deep for words.

When we take upon ourselves this posture of sitting while Jesus prays, we allow ourselves to enter and experience the mystery of the intimate presence of the Spirit praying within us, penetrating, speaking and holding us in our sorrow. The emphasis here isn't on what we are doing but on what God is doing in us. Ultimately, we don't heal our sorrows. Rather, we posture ourselves in ways that allow God to heal us, to transform our sorrows into avenues of growth. This posture of sitting while Jesus prays reminds us that the Spirit is active and speaking. Our part is to learn to sit, yielding to God's activity in us, opening ourselves to his healing power, listening to the silent words.

The trait that characterizes this posture of sitting is rest. To sit while Jesus prays is to relax and find our rest in God. "Rest in me," the Lord seems to be saying. "Rest in my prayer." And through our resting, we find healing for our sorrows.

When we are struggling with a sorrow, many of us have no idea how tired we are inside until we become still. Most of us have what I call "pockets of spiritual fatigue" within ourselves. Responding to pain and sorrow takes a lot of emotional and spiritual energy. Resting and sitting with the Lord needs to be a time of replenishing and restoring. Jesus promises us, "Come to me, all you who labor and are overburdened, and I will give you rest" (Matt 11:28). However, in the drivenness of our society, it's difficult to make time to be quiet and to rest in the Lord in this way. But if we allow ourselves to have the freedom to do this, we will find the healing for our sorrows that we so much desire.

The Greek word for rest is *hesychia*, a term that also came to mean praying. Hesychasm was a way of unceasing prayer in which a person descended into the heart and built a nest for oneself and God, a place where one rested in the Divine Presence, staying there throughout the day, throughout the pain, conflict, struggle, and sorrow. To sit while Jesus prays brings us to this kind of nesting in the heart. It allows us a replenishing rest in which we can be still and listen to the prayers and words that the Spirit whispers inside us. Julian of Norwich said that when a person is at ease or at rest with God, one "does not need to pray, but to contemplate reverently what God says."[4]

4. Norwich, *Showings*, 159.

Many times we do not know how to pray, or we simply don't have the strength for it. How wonderful it is to know that this is okay, because we can sit while he prays in us. We just need to give ourselves permission to rest. A young monk once asked Abba Moses, one of the desert fathers, how to find true spiritual growth. "Go, sit in your cell," said the monk, "and it will teach you everything."[5] Somehow we have lost this important secret in the spiritual life—that in "stayedness," as George Fox called it, we find healing for our sorrows. In the stayedness of resting we find everything we need in order to grow.

5. Merton, *Wisdom of the Desert*, 30.

4

Our Sorrows Lead Us to Deeper Compassion

IN OVER THIRTY YEARS as a psychotherapist, I have tried to help people deal with many different kinds of sorrows. For some, it has been the loss of a child or parent. For others, the sorrow has come from a broken relationship, an illness, the loss of a job, an addiction of some kind, a disappointment, or a problem within themselves that has been very difficult to overcome. What I have seen in my counseling is that some people mourn their sorrows and find ways to grow through them while others feel overwhelmed and end up "wasting their sorrows." Perhaps one of the most universal, positive rewards of dealing with sorrow for many is that it almost always leads people to be more compassionate and more understanding of other people and their struggles. This, then, becomes an avenue for spiritual and psychological growth and a way of using their own sorrow to help others.

Compassion begins with the acceptance of what is most human in ourselves and what is capable of most suffering. In attending to our own capacity to suffer, we can uncover a simple and profound connection between our own vulnerability and the vulnerability in others. Experiencing this allows us to find an instinctive kindness toward life which is the foundation of all compassion and genuine service.

After a dozen years, Alzheimer's disease had virtually destroyed Linda's brain, erasing her memories and with them all of her sense of who she was. Confined to a nursing home, she was adrift and frightened, given to pacing back and forth in a seemingly endless fashion filled with a nameless anxiety. Such repetitive pacing is common in people at the last stages of this disease, almost as if they are being driven to search for something hopelessly lost.

All the staff's efforts to ease her fear had failed. For a long time she was at rest only when she slept and her unending movement had caused her to become painfully thin. Then one day, quite by accident, as she passed the full-length mirror that hung to the left of the door to the courtyard, she caught sight of her own reflection in the glass. Becoming still for the first time in many months, she stood before it, fascinated, an odd expression on her face. She looked as if she had just met a friend from long ago, someone whose face was vaguely familiar but whose connection to oneself cannot be immediately recalled.

As a result of her disease, Linda had not spoken in many months. But drawn to the image in the mirror, for reasons long forgotten, she began to speak to it in a language all her own. Day after day she would stand and talk to the woman in the mirror for hours on end. It made her calm.

The nurses welcomed this new behavior with relief. Her endless pacing and anxiety had made her very difficult to care for. Accustomed to much random, senseless behavior on the part of their patients, they paid little further attention to how she now spent her time. But her doctor saw this differently. Every day on his rounds, he would stop at the mirror and spend some time with her. Standing next to her, he too would talk to the woman in the mirror with his usual kindness and respect. Once, at the end of one of his longer chats with Linda's reflection, he was deeply moved to notice that Linda had tears in her eyes. The nurses were deeply moved as well. Unable to cure his patient's brutal disease, this compassionate physician instinctively strengthened her last connection to herself with his simple presence and validated her worth as a human being.[1]

For Linda, who saw herself in the mirror, it was like meeting someone that she had known a long time ago. Gradually, she was able to speak to herself in the mirror in a language all her own. It was like coming home to herself.

Meister Eckhart was adamant that compassion was the aim of all spiritual growth. "If you were in an ecstasy as deep as that of St. Paul and there was a sick man who needed a cup of soup, it were better for you that you returned from the ecstasy and brought the cup of soup for love's sake."[2]

What does it mean to become more compassionate? And how do our sorrows allow this dimension of our personalities to emerge? The answer becomes clear when we look at the word *compassion*, which literally means "with" (*com-*) "suffering" (*passion*). To have compassion is to suffer with. It is not feeling a detached pity but sharing the pain with someone else. Compassion allows us to have empathy for another person. Thomas Kelly put it beautifully: "One might say we become cosmic mothers tenderly caring for all."[3] Becoming a "cosmic mother" is very similar to Charles de Foucald's idea of being a "universal brother or sister." It means to relate to the world in such a way that we see others not as strangers but as part of us. This relatedness allows us to walk with them in their deep and wounded places.

In Robert Coles' account of meeting Dorothy Day, he recalled that Dorothy was sitting at a table with a woman who was obviously very drunk. At first, Coles thought this was very strange—that she would be wasting her time trying to talk with a woman who could hardly speak coherently. But as he watched her, he could tell that Dorothy was trying to be present to this lady, which left a remarkable impression on him. Even though she was drunk, Dorothy paid attention to her. She had noticed her. For that moment, at least,

1. Remen, *My Grandfather's Blessings*, 103–4.
2. LeShan, *How to Meditate*, 92.
3. Kelly, *A Testament of Devotion*, 99.

Dorothy had clothed her with respect. She had walked with her in her deep and wounded life. Hers was a compassionate presence.

Morrie Schwartz, in *Tuesdays with Morrie*, said he would not have been the man he was without the years he spent working at a mental hospital just outside Washington, DC—a place with the deceptively peaceful name of Chestnut Lodge. It was one of Morrie's first jobs after finishing his PhD from the University of Chicago. Having rejected medicine, law, and business, Morrie had decided that the research world would be a place where he could contribute to others without exploiting them.

Morrie was given a grant to observe mental patients and record their treatments. While this idea seems common today, it was groundbreaking in the early fifties. Morrie saw some patients who would scream all day and others who would cry all night; patients soiling their underwear; patients refusing to eat, having to be held down, medicated, and fed intravenously.

One of the patients, a middle-aged woman, came out of her room every day and lay face down on the tile floor. She would stay there for hours as doctors and nurses stepped around her. No one hardly noticed her anymore and certainly no one paid much attention to her. Morrie watched in horror. He took notes, which is what he was there to do. Every day, she did the same thing: came out in the morning, lay on the floor, stayed there until the evening, talking to no one, ignored by everyone. It saddened Morrie. He began to sit on the floor with her, even lie down alongside her, trying to draw her out of her misery. Eventually, he got her to sit up and even return to her room. They were gradually becoming friends. What she mostly wanted, he learned, was the same thing most people want: someone to pay attention to her and notice that she was there.[4]

Another woman, who would spit at everyone else, took to Morrie and called him her friend. They talked each day, and the staff was at least encouraged that someone had gotten through to her.

---

4. Albom, *Tuesdays with Morrie*, 109–10.

Morrie observed that most of the patients there had been rejected and ignored in their lives, made to feel that they didn't exist, just like the drunk lady that Dorothy spent time with. Having a compassionate person "who notices that we are there" and "clothes us with respect" is a healing grace for everyone in life. To believe that we are truly special and important brings a peace that is life-giving.

Once divine compassion takes hold of us, we can never be the same again. We are compelled to suffer with, wait with, cry with those around us. We want to "take the pain out" of those who are homeless, the hungry, the abused, the rejected, the poor, the lonely, the sick, the grieving, the fragmented, the worn down, the defeated, and the oppressed as much as we can. We do it for no reason except that compassion asks it.

Meister Eckhart also said that love "has no why."[5] We can't always separate out our motives and respond purely from love. There can often be hidden agendas that grow out of the little game we play of "what's in it for me." Yet real compassion flows from God within—from plenitude, not ego or neediness. Such compassion is always born from within, not imposed or mandated from without.

We know that Jesus was walking, talking compassion. Many stories in the New Testament attest to this. As we become more compassionate, we become more like Christ, showing an uncanny interest in the poor, the excluded, the disenfranchised, the "least of my brothers." Then, we find ourselves sitting by our Samaritan well, more interested in breaking down barriers than in religious do's and don'ts. We wrap a towel around our waist and serve one another. We come to the rescue of others, like Jesus with the adulterous woman about to be stoned, as we try to bind up the wounds around us and do our small part to create community and justice for everyone.

Besides our individual sorrows and suffering, there is also a collective suffering that is difficult to comprehend. It can evoke a level of compassion that can be overwhelming. It can also make

5. Fox, *Breakthrough*, 206.

us feel helpless. This level of suffering is exemplified in a story I read some years ago. In the 1980s, a psychologist who lived and practiced in New York City decided to attend a two-day professional workshop based on several short films of one of Carl Jung's last pupils, the great Jungian dream analyst Marie-Louise von Franz. Between the showing of these films, a distinguished panel consisting of the heads of two major Jungian training centers and Carl Jung's own grandson responded to written questions from the audience sent up to the stage on cards.

One of these cards told the story of a horrific recurring dream, in which the dreamer was stripped of all human dignity and worth through Nazi atrocities. A member of the panel read the dream out loud. As he listened, the psychologist began to formulate a dream interpretation in his head, in anticipation of the panel's response. It was really a "no-brainer," he thought, as his mind busily offered his symbolic explanation for the torture and atrocities described in the dream. But this was not how the panel responded at all. When the reading of the dream was complete, Jung's grandson looked out over the large audience. "Would you all please rise?" he asked. "We will stand together in a moment of silence in response to this dream." As the audience stood for a minute, the psychologist waited impatiently for the discussion that he was certain would follow. But when they sat again, the panel went on to the next question.

The psychologist simply did not understand this at all, and a few days later he asked one of his teachers, himself a Jungian analyst, about it. "Bob," he said, "there is in life a suffering so unspeakable, a vulnerability so extreme that it goes far beyond words, beyond explanations and even beyond healing. In the face of such suffering, all we can really do is bear witness so no one need suffer alone."

In his book *Night,* famous author and concentration camp survivor Elie Wiesel wrote about this kind of collective suffering with his horrifying childhood experiences in a Nazi concentration camp. Having gone without food and drink for three days, thousands of Jews were driven out of their barracks at dawn into a thickly falling snow and herded into a field. Forbidden to sit or even move very much, they stood in line until evening, waiting for a train that would take them deeper into Germany. The snow drifted in a layer on their shoulders.

Finally, their thirst became intolerable. One man suggested that they eat the snow, but the guards would not allow them to bend over. The person in front of that man agreed to let him eat the snow that had accumulated on the back of his shoulders. That act spread through the line until there, in a frozen field, what had been individuals struggling with their separate pain became a community sharing their sufferings together.[6]

A compassionate heart understands that we will survive as a human family only as we are willing, one by one, to become a place of nourishment for our brother and sister. We will survive as we cease being individuals struggling alone with our sorrows and instead become a community sharing our sorrows in a great collective act of compassion.

Closer to home, so to speak, but still very much another example of collective suffering, is what I experience every week volunteering at the Franciscan Center in a very poor section of downtown Baltimore. In the face of the sorrows of these people, I must admit that I often ask myself why I am doing this. In the long run, what difference is this going to make for so many people who suffer every day with overwhelming sorrows? Then, I remember two things. The first is what Jesus told his disciples in Matthew's Gospel: "For I was hungry and you gave me food; I was thirsty and you gave me drink; I was a stranger and you made me welcome; naked and you clothed me, sick and you visited me, in prison and you came to see me . . . I tell you solemnly, in so far as you did this to one of the least of these brothers of mine, you did it to me" (Matt 25:35–40). Realizing this helps me stay motivated to continue volunteering.

The second thing I remember is a story about starfish. It seems as though there was an elderly man who used to walk along a beach at low tide, picking up starfish drying in the sun and gently throwing them back into the ocean. He had been doing this for

6. Wiesel, *Night*, 109.

some time when a jogger overtook him and asked him what he was doing. The old man explained that the starfish would die in the sun, and so he was throwing them back into the ocean. Astounded, the younger man began to laugh. "Why, old fellow, don't waste your time. Can't you see that there are hundreds and hundreds of starfish on this beach? And thousands of beaches in this world? And another low tide tomorrow? What makes you think that you can make a difference?" Still laughing, he ran on down the beach.

The old man watched him for a long time. Then he walked on and before long he passed another starfish. Stooping, he picked it up and looked at it thoughtfully. Then, gently, he threw it back into the ocean. "Made a difference to that one," he said to himself.

Sometimes, we can become so caught up in and overwhelmed by the problems in our world, our society, and our communities that we don't remember that our work is not about changing society—a world we cannot completely change. Rather, it's about touching the lives that touch mine in a way that makes a difference.

The Dalai Lama has said that "compassion occurs only between equals." For those who have compassion, woundedness is not a place of judgment but a place of genuine meeting.

Sometimes, when a life of service involves working with situations in which there are no easy answers, what we find there is so overwhelming that our hearts can break. We might think that, compared to the size of the problem, what we do means very little. But this is simply not the case. When it comes down to it, no matter how great or how small the need, we can only bless one life at a time.

Perhaps the final step in the healing of all wounds is the discovery of our capacity for compassion. This is like possessing an intuitive knowledge that all living beings are vulnerable to loss and sorrow. It is only in the presence of compassion that we can share our wounds without diminishing our wholeness.

One time, the director of an adolescent clinic in New York City was asked how he could continue the work year after year when the kids he saw had so many social problems that nothing he did could make a difference. "Why, no," he replied with conviction.

"With kids like these, *everything* I do makes a difference." It all depends on your perspective. It all depends on your attitude and the way you see things.

Oscar Romero, the former archbishop of El Salvador, was a champion of the poor. Reflecting on his work and wanting to encourage others to become more involved in working with the poor, he inspired the quote, "We cannot do everything, and there is a sense of liberation in realizing that. This enables us to do something, and to do it very well. It may be incomplete, but it is a beginning, a step along the way, an opportunity for the Lord's grace to enter and do the rest."[7]

7. Untener, "Archbishop Oscar Romero Prayer."

5

Our Sorrows Help Us Become a Blessing to Others

As I have become older, I have realized that when life is stripped down to its very essentials, it is surprising how simple things become. Fewer and fewer things matter, and those that matter, matter a great deal more.

In over thirty years of counseling, I have learned a great deal about blessing and serving life from the people that I have seen in my office. I have seen so many of them emerge from their encounter with great sorrow more compassionate and altruistic than before. Perhaps this is because their sorrows force people so deeply into their own vulnerability that they can identify with the vulnerability of others. Perhaps it is because through their own sorrows they have come to understand at a very deep level that not "wasting their sorrows" is one of the dimensions of life that matter a great deal to them. They want to use their sorrows in a positive way by becoming a blessing to others.

As we become more compassionate, we want to become more of a blessing to others through a life of service in whatever ways are possible for us. Some years ago, a patient shared one of her early struggles with me. When she was younger, she said that it had taken her a long time to realize that she had an impact on the people around her. For years, she suffered from shyness and a lack of self-esteem. She felt as though she was invisible to others and that her presence or absence had little or no influence on anyone. As a young adult, she would often not respond to a written invitation or return a phone message. Sometimes she would leave a party without a word to anyone, including the host or hostess. It simply never occurred to her that anyone might notice that she had not responded or that she was no longer there. Years later, she was stunned to discover that all those years she had been seen as aloof and rude and that her behavior often hurt people. Because she felt so badly about herself, she truly believed that her presence didn't matter.

Many people do not know that they can be an important blessing to others. Like my patient, they don't realize how much their presence matters to others. They don't know that they can strengthen or diminish the life around them. The way they live each day simply may not reflect back to them their power to influence the lives of others. But it is important to realize that we all have the power to affect others. We can affect those we hardly know and even those we do not know at all. Many of the people I have worked with over the years have been taken completely by surprise by this power.

Without our realizing it, we may influence the lives of others in very simple ways. When Emily became ill many years ago, bulimia was not yet a household word. Filled with guilt at her uncontrollable behavior, she had been taken to specialist after specialist until someone was able to identify the problem as something more than teenage rebellion. She had been hospitalized for a year and this had saved her life. Slowly, she fought her way back from the edge, surrounded by concerned adults who could not understand why she was bringing this on herself. She did not understand it either.

As she described it to me, "I just felt so *alone*. I could not stop myself, and at the worst of it I was not sure that it was possible to survive this. I was very afraid. I remember thinking that somewhere there must be someone else who has this problem, someone who has been able to heal from it. If they could live, maybe I could live too." At the time, Emily had not met another person with bulimia, but after many years of difficulty she had somehow found her own way through this illness and was able to recover. She could not really explain why.

A few years ago, she was reading her evening newspaper and came across an announcement for a meeting of a bulimia support group. Emily was a middle-aged woman by this time and had not suffered from this problem for many years, but the idea of a support group intrigued her, and so she decided to attend a meeting to see what it was like. It had been a powerful experience. The desperately ill young people there had touched her heart and, while she felt unable to help them, she cared about them and continued going back. Other than saying she had bulimia as a girl, she did not reveal a great deal more about herself but simply sat and listened to the stories of others.

As she was about to leave one of these meetings, she was stopped by a painfully thin young girl who thanked her for coming and told her how much it had meant to know her. The girl's eyes were filled with tears. Emily responded with her usual graciousness, but she had been puzzled. She could not recall ever speaking to this girl and did not even know her name. As she drove home, she wondered how she could have forgotten something so important to someone else. She was almost home before she understood. Her husband, who met her at their front door, was surprised to see that she had been crying. "Emily, what is wrong?" he asked. "I have become the person I needed to meet, Harry," she told him as she walked into the house.

Sometimes our presence shines through us, even when we are not aware of it. We become a blessing to others simply by being who we are.

It is also possible to affect people's lives in major ways through very minor actions. A colleague who is now happily married shared with me a single incident that freed her to change her life. She had been living for several years with a charming, highly educated man who was physically and psychologically abusive to her. He was deeply respected in the community, and to the outer world theirs was a perfect marriage. But their private life was something far different. Over and over, he told her that she had provoked him and had brought the abuse on herself by her stupidity and her other shortcomings. She would try even harder, but no matter how hard she tried she was never good enough. Over the years, she had become so frightened and uncertain of what was real that she had come to believe him.

All this changed one day on a street corner in New York City. As Elizabeth and her husband were standing at a crosswalk waiting for the light to change, she had looked across the street and noticed a building with beautiful modern architecture. She had called his attention to it. "Look Bill," she said, "isn't that building beautiful?" Thinking they were alone, he responded to her in the tone of absolute contempt that he reserved for their private conversations. "You mean the one over there that looks exactly like every other building on the street?" he sneered.

She flushed with shame and fell silent. And then a woman standing next to them, a complete stranger who was also waiting for the light to change, turned and glared at him. "She's absolutely right, you know," she said with a strong New York accent. "That building is beautiful. And you, sir, are a horse's ass." When the light turned green, this woman crossed the street and walked away.

It was the defining moment in the relationship, my colleague told me. Suddenly, everything became crystal clear. She knew then that she would find the strength to leave him. It would take some time, but she knew she could do it.

To recognize your capacity to affect life is to know yourself deeply and to recognize your real value and power, independent of any role that you have been given to play or expertise you may have acquired. It is possible to strengthen or diminish the life around you in almost any role.

In order for us not to be a "waster of sorrows," we need to learn how to become a blessing to others. The capacity to bless life is in everybody and most of us bless life far more than we realize. Many simple, ordinary things that we do can affect those around us in profound ways: the unexpected phone call, the brief touch, the willingness to listen, the warm smile. We can even bless total strangers and be blessed by them.

Blessings can come in the form of a greeting commonly used in India. On meeting even a total stranger, one bows and says, "*Namaste*": I see the divine spark within you. Often we are fooled by someone's appearance—their age or illness or anger or meanness—or just too busy to recognize that there is in everyone a place of goodness and integrity, no matter how deeply buried it might be. Sometimes we are too hurried or distracted to stop and see it. But when we recognize this spark of God in others, we have the opportunity to touch the unborn goodness in them and encourage them to use their goodness to help others.

A blessing is really about seeing the spark of God in one another. God may not need our attention as badly as the person next to us on the bus or behind us in line at the grocery store. But everyone in the world matters and so do their blessings. And even as we grow older, it is important to understand that the power of our blessing is not diminished by illness or age. On the contrary, our blessings can become even more powerful because they have survived the buffeting of our years and experience. Our blessings have incorporated the sorrows we have experienced in life. And although we may have traveled a long, difficult road to get to the place where our sorrows can give hope to others, we also hope that in time they too will be able to arrive at this place beyond competition and struggle, where we belong to one another.

Finally, a blessing is not something that one person simply gives another. A blessing is a "moment of meeting," a certain kind of relationship in which both people involved remember and acknowledge their true nature and worth. This moment of meeting allows them to strengthen what is whole in one another. It is then that they offer each other a place of refuge from an indifferent world.

Those who bless and serve life find a place of belonging and strength, a refuge from living in ways that are meaningless and empty and lonely. Blessing life moves us closer to each other and closer to our authentic selves. When people are blessed, they discover that their lives matter and that there is something in them worthy of blessing. It brings them closer to their own goodness. And when you bless others, you may discover this same thing is also true about yourself.

The thirty-five years that I have been a psychotherapist have shown me that any of the ordinary aspects of our lives—our joys, our failures, our loves, our losses, and our sorrows—can become a blessing to others. I have seen people use almost anything to bless life. There is such a simple goodness in all of us that nothing should be wasted.

6

Our Sorrows Lead Us to Service

As we grow in compassion and want to become more of a blessing to others, we find that serving others becomes more a part of our lives. It's not simply doing this or that thing for someone. Rather, service becomes a basic stance for us in life that finds many different avenues of expression. For some, it might mean helping someone in need on a regular basis. For others, it will be helping someone as the need arises each day. For still others, it might mean volunteering with some organization that is dedicated to helping others. Whatever expression our service takes, it always does something to us personally.

Flying back from Florida a week before Christmas, a friend found herself seated in a section of the plane completely taken over by over a dozen young boys and their parents who were returning from a national baseball tournament. Their team had come in second place and emotions were high. So was the noise level. Seated next to my friend was a very heavy woman with a cranky two-year-old. She seemed to be planning to hold this child on her lap all the way to San Francisco. However, this did not strike him as a great idea, and he let her know this at the top of his voice! My friend asked the flight attendant if she could change seats, but there was none available. Since reading or doing any kind of work was out of the question, my friend started a conversation with this lady, asking her about the baseball league. She began to tell her story about the time she spends with the team, the hours of cheering them on, of going door to door to raise money for equipment and travel, and why she was here now with two of her sons. She went on to say that in her neighborhood many boys were dead or locked away by aged twenty, victims of drugs or violence. This baseball league was her life insurance for her kids. My friend listened to her with new respect.

Then, this lady asked my friend about her own life. Since my friend was a cancer survivor and was working in this area, she shared some of the struggles related to this illness. As this lady listened, a sadness filled her eyes and she began to tell my friend about her neighbor, a woman like herself, a single mother with four little kids. Six months ago she had been diagnosed with cancer. "The chemo she has to take is terrible," the lady said. "It makes her so sick, sometimes she can hardly get out of bed. I sure hope she can make it through this."

As she continued to share this story, my friend began to wonder how she knew so many details of her neighbor's life. So she asked her that question. The lady's answer stunned her. When that tragedy had struck next door, she had simply moved her neighbor and all her children into her own home. They had been there for the past five months. My friend said that she looked at her closely. There was not the slightest air of martyrdom or self-congratulation about her, just this natural reaching out to a person in trouble whose life was next to her own.

This was compassion leading to service. This was a lady who had become a wonderful blessing to this mother with cancer and her four children. This lady possessed a basic stance in life of wanting to help others, and acted when she saw the need.

If we have this basic stance in life to be of service whenever the need arises, we will find that there are many opportunities to help others, even when we least expect it. Sometimes we won't even realize it at the time. But the Lord will use us in a variety of ways.

Rachel Naomi Remen recounts Father O'Shea's story about the first patient he had been called to see as a hospital chaplain:

Very young and desperate to be of service, he had gone to visit a woman who was facing major surgery the following morning. She was lying in her bed, tense with anxiety. He had no sooner pulled up a chair when she told him, "Father, I feel certain that I am going to die tomorrow."

Nothing in his training had prepared him for this, and he had sat there with absolutely no idea of how to respond. To cover his confusion, he had reached out and taken her hand. She had then begun to talk. Still holding her hand and barely listening, he had reached back in his mind for some of the great words of comfort from his tradition, the words of Merton, Teresa D'Avila, of Jesus. He had them all with him when he had entered the room but somehow now they were gone.

The woman continued to talk and even to cry a little, and his heart went out to her in her fear. At last she closed her eyes, and he took the opportunity to ask God for help, for the words that he needed. But he had found no words at all. Eventually she had simply fallen asleep and he had left, vanquished, deflated, convinced that he was not cut out to be a priest. He had spent the rest of the day and most of the night in an agonizing assessment of his shortcomings and his calling. He had been too ashamed to visit her again.

But a few weeks later he had received a note from her, thanking him for all he had done for her during his visit, and most especially for all the wonderful things he had told her, words of comfort and wisdom. She would never forget them. And then she quoted some of what she had heard him say, at length.

Father O'Shea began to laugh, and I did, too. "It was so long ago," he chuckled. "Thank goodness we can never be that young again." He paused for a moment to wipe his eyes. "You know, Rachel, he told me. "Over the years I have learned that when I pray to be able to be of service to someone, sometimes God says 'Yes' and sometimes God says 'No,' but quite often God says, 'Step aside, Patrick. I'll do it myself.'"[1]

---

1. Remen, *My Grandfather's Blessings*, 331–32.

Sometimes we may think that we are serving others in one way and later discover that we have been serving them in quite another. We might not even realize it at the time. A doctor shared his experience as a fellow on a large inner-city AIDS ward. It was some years ago, before protease inhibitors and other drug therapies were available, and many of the patients who were admitted to his care died. Most of them were young men, very close to his own age—people that he deeply cared about. After a few months of this, he became overwhelmed by a sense of futility and became quite depressed.

This doctor happened to be a Buddhist, and it had always been his practice to pray for his patients. When a patient died, he would light a candle on his altar at home, pray for each person daily, and keep it burning for a month. Reflecting on his service many years later, he said that he had begun to wonder that perhaps the reason he was there was not what he had thought. He had expected to serve by trying to cure his patients. When their problems proved resistant to his medical expertise, he had felt useless. But maybe he was not meant to be there to cure people. Perhaps he was there so that no one would die without someone to pray for them. Perhaps he had served every one of his patients more than he would ever know.

Basically, service is about letting the lives that touch yours touch you, as this doctor had wanted to do for his patients. These days, many people seem to think that being touched is a form of weakness. Not only have we disconnected from life, but many of us have disconnected from each other as well. Such qualities as self-reliance, self-determination, and self-sufficiency are so deeply admired among us that needing someone is often seen as a personal failure. Needing others has come to almost require an act of courage. It is not surprising that so many people are secretly lonely and afraid. Perhaps it is this striving for excessive independence that makes so many of us vulnerable to isolation, cynicism, and depression.

It is doubtful that independence and individualism will ultimately enable us to live in the deepest and most fulfilling way. This is because in order for us to grow spiritually and psychologically, we need to be able to know and trust one another. We need to allow ourselves to touch and be touched by those around us. Service is one of the ways that we can heal from our sorrows in life and help to take the pain out of things.

True service is not a relationship between an expert and a problem. It is far more genuine than that. It is a mutual relationship between people who are willing to generously share their humanity with each other. Service goes beyond any expertise that we might possess. Service is actually another way of life.

With all of our best intentions, it can also be true that many times when we help we might not really serve. Those who help see life differently from those who serve, and may affect life differently as well. It is difficult not to see the person you are helping as someone weaker than yourself, someone more needy. This was the way it was for me when I first began to volunteer at the Franciscan Center. I certainly thought I was going there to help people who were very needy. After all, I thought, this place is in a very poor area of Baltimore. I was helping to feed over four hundred very needy people every Wednesday. This was clearly helping the needy, I thought. In a sense, this was true. However, over the years, I have come to understand that when we serve there are other things happening. When we help, we become aware of our strength because we are using it. Others become aware of our strength as well and may feel diminished by it. What I have come to understand is that we do not simply serve with our strength. We serve with our whole person. We draw from all our experiences, including our sorrows. Over the years, I have discovered that everything I know serves and everything I am serves. I have served others with my own strengths and my weaknesses as well as my sorrows. I have come to see that service is a relationship between equals.

As I have served, I have also become aware of my own wholeness and have become more accepting of it. In using it to serve, I have come to see and understand its power. Many times my own limitations and sorrows have become the source of my compassion. My own wounds have made me gentle with the wounds of other people and helped me learn to trust the mysterious process by which we can heal. My own loneliness has made me able to recognize the loneliness in others, to respect the place where everyone is alone and meet others in the dark. Maybe most humbling of all, I have found that sometimes the thing that serves best is not all my hard-earned psychological knowledge but something about life I may have learned from my clients or from a child.

I have also learned that a helping relationship may incur a sense of debt, but service, like healing, is mutual. Service is free from debt. The wholeness in me is strengthened just like the wholeness in you. Everyone has the opportunity to participate. In helping, we may find a sense of satisfaction. In serving, we have an experience of gratitude.

Serving is also different from fixing. Abraham Maslow said, "it is tempting, if all you have have is a hammer, to treat everything as if it were a nail."[2] Seeing yourself as a fixer may cause you to see brokenness everywhere and to sit in judgment on life itself. Fixers trust their own experience. When we fix others, we may not see their hidden wholeness or trust the integrity of the life in them. But when we serve, we see the unborn wholeness in others. We collaborate with it and strengthen it. Then others may be able to see their own wholeness for the first time.

Perhaps fixing is only a way to relate to things. But to relate to another human being in this way is to deny and diminish in some profound and subtle way the power of the life in them and its mystery. For over forty years I have been helped and fixed in a variety of ways by many people. I am grateful to them all. But all that helping and fixing left me wounded in some important and fundamental ways. Only service heals.

Everyone who serves, serves life. What we serve is something worthy of our presence, our attention, and the commitment of our time and our lives. Serving is not about fixing life, outwitting life, manipulating life, controlling life, or struggling to gain mastery over life. When we serve, we discover that life itself is holy.

2. Maslow, *Psychology of Science*, ch. 2.

Finally, service is closer to generosity than it is to duty. It connects us to one another and to life itself. When we experience our connectedness with others, serving them becomes the natural and joyful thing to do. Over the long run, fixing and helping are draining but service is renewing. When you serve, your work itself will sustain you, renew you, and bless you, often over many years.

Albert Schweitzer said, "I don't know what your destiny will be, but one thing I know: the only ones among you who will be really happy are those who have sought and found how to serve."[3] Maybe this is truly the way to discover real happiness in life. Why? Because service is the lived experience of belonging. It is the final healing of isolation and loneliness.

3. Quoted from the website of Albert Schweitzer's Leadership for Life, at http://aschweitzer/abouta.html.

7

Our Sorrows Allow Us to Become "a Lap," a Place of Refuge for Each Other

IN MY COUNSELING PRACTICE, I have learned that denial, anger, and rationalization are some of the common ways that people deal with suffering and sorrow. But few of these are places of refuge. Most of these coping mechanisms will disconnect us from the very life we hope to live and can undermine our health in a variety of ways. However, the sad part of this is that we can never hide from suffering and sorrow. They are a part of being alive. Hiding ourselves means only that we will have to suffer alone.

In the presence of our sorrows, everyone needs to find a place of refuge. A friend once told me that a highly skilled AIDS doctor named Vicki keeps a picture of her grandmother in her home and sits before it for a few minutes every day before she leaves for work. Her grandmother was an Italian-born woman who was very close to her family. She was also a very wise woman. When Vicky was very small, her kitten was killed in an accident. It was her first experience of death and she was devastated. Her parents encouraged her not to be sad, telling her that her kitten was in heaven now with God. Despite these assurances, she was not comforted. She prayed to God, asking him to give her kitten back, but God did not respond.

In her sorrow, she turned to her grandmother and asked, "Why?" Her grandmother did not tell her that her kitten was in heaven, like so many other adults had done. Instead, she simply held her and reminded her of the time when her grandfather had died. She too had prayed to God, but God had not brought grandpa back. She did not know why. Vicky laid her head on her grandmother's shoulder and sobbed. When she was finally able to look up, she saw that her grandmother was crying as well.

Although her grandmother could not answer her questions, a great sadness had been lifted and she felt able to go on. All the assurances that Whiskers was in heaven had not given her this strength or peace. "My grandmother was a lap," Vicky said, "a place of refuge." This doctor knew a great deal about AIDS, but what she really wanted to be for her patients was a "lap," a place from which they could face what they had to face and not be alone.

Facing into our own sorrows and trying to deal with them in constructive ways allows us to become "a lap, a place of refuge" for others. Sometimes the deepest healing comes from the natural fit between two wounded people's lives.

Besides being a place of refuge for others, we also need to find places of refuge for our own sorrows. Sometimes this can be even more difficult. Some might look on this as a weakness, but it is really a strength. Taking refuge does not mean hiding from life. It means finding a place of strength, the capacity to live the life we have been given with greater courage. This is one of the things that our friends do for us. With them, we can find a place of refuge, a lap to rest in. With them, we can find a person with whom we can share our sorrows and find the strength to go on. Because they know us so well, and because we trust them to be there for us, we can share our sorrows and find healing. Sometimes, simply being known and accepted as we are and cared about by others can affect us in very profound ways.

Another way to find a place of refuge for ourselves is to develop what we might call "personal renewal zones." These renewal zones protect us. They provide us with a respite, a place for inner refreshment and renewal. They provide space for us to be free, to be ourselves. If we don't have such spaces, our sorrows at times can overwhelm us and make coping with the realities of everyday living more difficult. If you don't already have any personal renewal zones in your life, you might try the following to see if they might help.

- quiet walks by yourself
- time and space for meditation
- spiritual and recreational reading, including the diaries and biographies of others you admire
- exercise
- associating with cheerful friends
- enjoying a hobby
- phone calls to family and friends who inspire and tease you
- involvement in projects that renew
- listening to music you enjoy

Personal renewal zones can be very helpful, then, if we are to integrate our sorrows in life in a positive way. They help to refresh us and can lead to healing. Availing ourselves of these types of activities that truly renew us can be places of refuge for us.

Sometimes a church or various groups, organizations, and communities can also be places of refuge for us. Hospice, for example, is often this for people who are dying, as well as their families. At a very important and vulnerable time, hospice volunteers bring peace and comfort during a person's final journey. The organization Compassionate Friends is a support group for people who have lost a loved one. They were clearly a place of refuge for me and my wife after our first child, a son, was stillborn. His death caused a tremendous sorrow for us. It's the kind of sorrow that I believe you don't ever really get over. You just try to grieve, to cope as best you can and continue on. As we were filled with sorrow and grief, these people provided a safe place to grieve. They became "a lap, a place of refuge" for us. They gave us the freedom to feel all the emotions that accompany this kind of loss and set us on a path to healing. We have always been grateful to them.

We can avoid suffering and sorrow only at the great cost of distancing ourselves from life. In order to live fully, we need to look deeply and respectfully at our own sorrows and at the sorrows of others. In the depths of every wound we have survived is the strength we need to live. The wisdom our sorrows can offer us is a place of refuge. Finding this is not for the faint of heart. But then, neither is life.

8

Pay Attention to the Wisdom
of Our Sorrows

THE STRUGGLE TO FIND meaning in our sorrows can be very challenging. Usually it does not require us to live differently; it requires
us to see our lives differently. Many of us already live far more
meaningful lives than we know. When we go beyond the super-
ficial to the essential, things that are familiar and even common-
place are revealed in new ways. But discovering this takes time
and patience. It requires a wisdom that often comes from living
with and struggling with our sorrows. If we can learn this wisdom
about life, it will allow us to never be a "waster of sorrows."

Finding meaning in our sorrows changes the way we see ourselves and the world. Through our sorrows we come to know ourselves for the first time and recognize not only who we genuinely
are but also what truly matters to us. As a psychotherapist, I have
accompanied many people as they have discovered in themselves
an unexpected strength, a courage beyond what they would have
thought possible, an unsuspected sense of compassion, or a capacity for love deeper than they had ever dreamed. I have watched
people abandon values that they had never before questioned and
find courage to live in new ways.

When I first met Kathy, her psychology practice was barely
surviving. She shared offices with a group of physicians, and,

desperate to be accepted and work under what she perceived as the umbrella of their credibility, she took whatever crumbs fell from their professional table. Hers was the smallest office in the complex, and her name was the only one not listed on the office door. It was obvious from the beginning how dedicated and gifted she was as a therapist. However, her compromising attitude troubled me, although I didn't say anything about it at the time. But Kathy felt validated by the association and she was convinced that she needed referrals from the doctors in order to have patients.

Kathy was a shy person, a little apologetic and sometimes hesitant in trying to find the right words in a conversation. She was also just the slightest bit clumsy. However, all this actually made her very endearing. You felt somehow at home with her and safe. Her patients loved her.

One day she told me she was moving from her present office. Although I was pleased, I asked her why she had decided to leave. "They don't have wheelchair access," she said. I guess I looked surprised, because she went on to say that she had not told me everything about herself. She continued to tell her story and said that years ago when she was young, she had a very serious stroke and was not expected to recover. "I am astonished," I said. "I had no idea." She replied, "Nobody does." I went on to ask her why she had kept this part of her life a secret. Almost in tears, she said that for years she had felt damaged and ashamed. "I wanted to put it behind me," she said. "I thought if I could be seen as normal I would be more than I was." And so she had guarded her secret closely. Neither her colleagues nor her patients knew. She had felt certain that others would not refer to her or want to come to her for help if they knew. However, now she was no longer sure this was true.

"So, what do you plan to do now?" I asked her. She looked down at her hands in her lap. "I think I will just be myself," she told me. "I will see people like myself. People who are not like others. People who have had strokes and other brain injuries. People who can never be normal again. I think I can help them to be whole." Over the past five years, Kathy has become widely known for her work. She has been honored by several community groups and interviewed in newspapers. She often speaks on these kinds of topics and consults for businesses and hospitals. The many people she has helped refer others to her. Her practice is thriving. Her own name is on the door. All Kathy needed in order to be whole was the courage to face her own vulnerability. She had gradually learned to pay attention to the wisdom of her sorrow.

Life offers its wisdom generously to each of us. Everything in life teaches but not everyone learns. Life invites us to "Stay awake. Pay attention." But for most of us, paying attention is no simple matter. It requires us not to be distracted by expectations, past experiences, labels and masks. It asks that we not allow ourselves to jump to early conclusions and that we remain open to surprise. In fact, wisdom comes most easily to those who have the courage to embrace life without judgment. Sometimes it will require us to not know, even for a long time. Moreover, it will also require us to be more fully and simply alive than we have been taught to be. It may often require us to suffer. But ultimately it will lead to wisdom and growth.

There is a seed of greater wholeness in everyone. The great Christian mystic Meister Eckhart called this seed the Godseed. Buddhists call it the Buddha seed. Doctor Wayne Dyer calls this seed our "secret garden." It is that part of everyone that has the capacity for wisdom. Wisdom is not simply something that we acquire; it is something that we may become over time. It involves a change in our basic nature, a deepening of our capacity for compassion, loving-kindness, forgiveness, and service. Life itself waters this seed within us.

Knowing that a Godseed is present in everyone changes the way you see things. Many things are more than they seem. Many things do not wear their true nature on their sleeve. For example, what you can see and touch about an acorn—its color, its weight, and its hardness—will never hint at the secret of its potential. This secret is not directly measurable but, given the proper conditions over time, it will become visible.

Within an acorn, there is something waiting to unfold that will become an oak tree. An acorn is defined by this capacity.

Something can be the size, shape, weight, texture, and color of an acorn, but without this hidden power to become an oak tree, it is not an acorn. In the same way, our essential humanity is defined by this Godseed in us, this capacity to grow in wisdom.

Every acorn yearns toward the full expression of its nature and uses every opportunity to realize its capacity to become an oak tree. Similarly, there is a natural yearning toward wholeness and wisdom in us all as well. This varies in strength from person to person. It may be quite conscious in some people and deeply buried in others. It may form the focus of one life and lie on the periphery of another, but it is always there. Wholeness is a basic human need.

None of us are born wise. Rather, it is a process and a struggle. Everyone and everything is caught up in this process of growing in wisdom, of becoming more transparent to what is going on within us and all around us. This struggle is to become free from our illusions and to grow in wisdom. But this is not usually a graceful or a deliberate process. We stumble forward, often in the dark, like the acorn, to become more of who we are. It is clearly an effort worthy of our patience, our support, our compassion, and our attention.

Possessing wisdom is very different from just having knowledge. Our life experiences can teach us this. When I was in graduate school, I studied very hard and learned how to be a therapist. Although it might sound simplistic, I truly wanted to help people and be the best possible therapist I could be. In class, I learned many theories of counseling and even had the opportunity of practicing them during my internships. I would meet a client, listen to them, establish rapport, diagnose them, decide what counseling strategy would be most beneficial, and go to work. I was putting my knowledge to work. The model I was taught focused on what I as a therapist had learned about this particular problem the person was experiencing, and supposedly gave me the tools, the strategies to help them. I was implementing my knowledge. But I didn't have much wisdom then. I was young and didn't have much life experience. What gave me some wisdom was the death of my son and my struggle through the years of trying to make sense of that reality. This experience enabled me to gradually understand so many things about loss, sorrow, life, and healing. In the final analysis, I believe this type of struggle enabled me to become a wise and helpful grief counselor for others. Even back then, I didn't want to be a "waster of sorrows."

Over the years, I have discovered in my counseling practice that, basically, I don't know what is needed much of the time and, even more surprising, I don't need to know. But now I also know that if I listen attentively to someone, to their essential self—their soul, as it were—I often find that, at their deepest level, they can sense the direction of their own healing and wholeness. If I can remain open to that, without expectations of what someone is "supposed to do," how they are supposed to change in order to "get better," or even what their wholeness looks like, what can happen is amazing. For me, this approach is much wiser and healthier than any way of fixing their situation or easing their pain and sorrow that I might devise on my own.

So I no longer have many theories about people. I don't simply diagnose them or decide what their problem is. I don't even believe that I have to fix them. I simply meet with them and listen. As we sit together, I don't even have an agenda, but I know that something will emerge from our conversation over time that is a part of a larger coherent pattern that neither of us can fully see at this moment. So I sit with them and wait.

The Celestine Prophecy offers a simple and helpful description of the possibility within all human relationships. It says that there is a way of relating to others that encourages a person to deliberately listen to the hidden beauty in themselves. The place of their beauty is often the place of their greatest integrity. When you listen, the integrity and wholeness in others moves closer together. Your presence and attention strengthens it and helps them to hear it in themselves. It has been my experience that presence and listening is a more powerful catalyst for change than analysis, and that we can know beyond doubt things we can never understand.

Many years ago, whenever I prepared for the final session with a client, I used to review in my mind the milestones and turning points in our work together that had led to their healing. I would come up with a list of these in which I played a rather central role. Carefully, I would go through my notes and document the insightful interventions I had made. But when I asked my clients themselves to talk about their own experience of healing, they would rarely come up with more than half of my list. The rest of the time, they would share things that surprised me—chance remarks and facial expressions of mine that they had interpreted in ways that evoked in them some important and liberating insight. Then they would give me examples of how they were able to use this insight to change their lives. Nodding sagely, I would often have no recollection of the event at all! Clearly, I had been used to delivering a message of healing to them that I did not fully understand at the time.

Learning from life takes time. Becoming wise usually takes a lot of time. Most of us rarely recognize life's wisdom at the time it is given. Sometimes we are too distracted by something else that has caught our wandering eye, and not every gift of wisdom comes nicely gift wrapped. I have often received such a gift only many years after it was offered. Sometimes I needed to receive other things first, to live through other experiences in order to be ready. Much wisdom is like a hand-me-down—it may be too big at the time it is given.

Similarly, gaining wisdom from our sorrows takes time. Writer and physician Rachel Remen invites us to look closely at the story of the oyster as a guide to seeking wisdom from hardships.

> An oyster is soft, tender, and vulnerable. Without the sanctuary of its shell it could not survive. But oysters must open their shells in order to "breathe" water. Sometimes while an oyster is breathing, a grain of sand will enter its shell and become a part of its life from then on.
>
> Such grains of sand cause pain, but an oyster does not alter its soft nature because of this. It does not become hard and leathery in order not to feel. It continues to entrust itself to the ocean, to open and breathe in order to live. But it does respond. Slowly and patiently, the oyster wraps the grain of sand in thin translucent layers

until, over time, it creates something of great value in the place where it was most vulnerable to its pain. A pearl might be thought of as an oyster's response to its pain and suffering. Not every oyster can do this. Oysters that do are far more valuable to people than oysters that do not.

Sand is a way of life for an oyster. If you are soft and tender and must live on the sandy floor of the ocean, learning to make pearls becomes a necessity if you are to survive and live well.[1]

We are all invited to grow in wisdom and learn how to integrate our sorrows. As we each do this in our own way, we slowly become a blessing to those around us and a light in our world. We will not become a "waster of sorrows." Perhaps the final step in the healing of our sorrows is wisdom. Perhaps no sorrow really heals completely until the wisdom of its experience has been found and appreciated. We will not return from the journey into sorrow to the same house that we left. Like the oyster, something in us has changed and the house that we return to and live in will be different as well.

Disappointment, loss, and sorrow are a part of everyone's life. Sometimes we can put these things behind us and get on with the rest of our lives. But not everything is amenable to this approach. Some things are too big or buried too deep within us to do this, and we will have to leave important parts of ourselves behind if we treat them in this way. These are the places where wisdom begins to grow in us. It begins with the suffering and sorrow that we do not avoid or rationalize or put behind us. It continues with the realization that our loss, our sorrow, whatever it is, has become a part of us and has altered our lives so profoundly that we cannot go back to the way it was before. Just like an oyster turns a grain of sand into a pearl, something in us can transform such loss and sorrow into wisdom. This process of turning sorrow into wisdom often looks like a sorting process. First, we experience everything. Then, one by one we let things go—the anger, the blame, the sense

1. Remen, *My Grandfather's Blessings*, 139–40.

of injustice, and finally even the pain itself—until all we have left is a deeper sense of the value of life and a greater capacity to live it. The grain of sand has become a pearl in us.

After thirty years of accompanying people as they deal with their sorrows, I would say that the experience of sorrow and the wisdom we find there will belong completely to each person in their own way. Often, it will help us to live better. Sometimes it may help us to die better as well.

9

Our Sorrows Help Us to Live with Mystery

PERHAPS ONE OF THE most difficult things in life to deal with is the unknown. This is certainly true about our sorrows. We want to know why something happens. We want to know the reason for things that happen to us. My wife and I desperately wanted to know why our son was stillborn. But there are no easy answers to these kinds of questions. They are part of the mystery of life.

The unknown in our lives is always difficult to handle constructively. Most of us are comfortable with what we know. It might be difficult to deal with the known in our lives but at least it doesn't generate the same kind of anxiety that dealing with the unknown does. As the eminent family therapist Virginia Satir said, "Most people prefer the certainty of misery to the misery of uncertainty."

One of my favorite quotes is from Rilke's *Letters to a Young Poet.* Writing to his young friend, he said,

> I beg you . . . to be patient toward all that is unsolved in your heart and try to love the questions themselves like locked rooms and like books that are written in a very foreign tongue. Do not seek the answers, which cannot be given to you because you would not be able to live them. And the point is, to live everything. Live the

question now. Perhaps you will then gradually, without
noticing it, live along some distant day into the answer.[1]

Mystery, by its very nature, cannot be solved, can never be
known. Many of us have not been raised to cultivate a sense of
mystery. In our society, it is particularly difficult to live with our
questions. We are trained to answer questions. We pride ourselves in solving the unknown. We like things fixed, figured out,
and nailed down. Some people even see our inability to solve the
unknown as an insult to our competence, almost a personal fail-
ing. Seen in this way, the unknown becomes a call to action. But
mystery does not require action; it requires our attention. Mystery
requires that we listen and become open. When we meet with the
unknown in this way, we can be touched by a wisdom that can
transform our lives.

Jesus was a master at using questions to invite people to grow.
"What are you looking for?" "Who do you say that I am?" "Do you
want to get well?" "Why do you not understand what I say?" "Do
you love me?" The New Testament is full of them.

There is an art to living your questions. You peel them. You
listen to them. You let them spawn new questions. You hold the
unknowing inside. You linger with them instead of rushing into
half-baked answers. Jesuit priest and writer Anthony De Mello put
it very well: "Some people will never learn anything because they
grasp too soon. Wisdom, after all, is not a station you arrive at, but
a manner of traveling. . . . To know exactly where you are headed
may be the best way to go astray. Not all who loiter are lost."[2]

As a matter of fact, those who "loiter" in the question long
enough will "live into" the answer. But we have to be patient. And
this waiting can be very difficult. Simone Weil said, "Waiting patiently in expectation is the foundation of the spiritual life."[3] Jesus
said, "search, and you will find" (Matt 7:7). Sometimes, I wonder if
this means, "Search *long enough*, and you will find." It is the patient

1. Rilke, *Letters to a Young Poet*, 35.
2. De Mello, *Heart of the Enlightened*, 38.
3. Weil, *First and Last Notebooks*, 99.

act of dwelling in the darkness of a question that eventually unravels the answer.

Everything and everyone possesses a dimension of the unknown. Mystery helps us to see ourselves and others from the largest possible perspective. To be living is to be unfinished. Nothing and no one is complete. The world and everything in it is *alive*. Reflecting on the importance of mystery in our lives, the well-known anthropologist Jane Goodall said, "How sad it would be . . . if we humans were to lose all sense of mystery, all sense of awe. If our left brains were utterly to dominate the right so that logic and reason triumphed over intuition and alienated us absolutely from our innermost being, from our hearts, our souls."[4]

A sense of mystery can take us beyond disappointment and judgment to a place of expectancy. It opens in us an attitude of listening and respect. This is what friends do for each other. A fellow questioner helps us learn how to *live* our questions instead of suppressing them. Emily Dickinson once wrote, "I dwell in possibility."[5] If everyone has in them the dimension of the unknown, possibility is present at all times. Wisdom then is possible at all times.

The important thing to remember is that mystery offers us the opportunity to wonder together and reclaim a sense of awe and aliveness. Even as a nation, if we lose our sense of mystery, we can become a nation of burned out people. But people who wonder do not burn out. Mystery reminds us to stay awake and listen, because the mystery at the heart of life may speak to us at any time. Living our way into the answers to our questions is an invitation to trust more deeply in the Lord's providence. It is believing that even though we cannot always discover satisfying answers to our questions, we know that there is a purpose to them. It is part of the mystery of our lives. And when part of the mystery involves not having answers to our questions that cause us sorrow, it is challenging and takes courage to accept the sorrows of our lives

4. Goodall, *Reason for Hope*, ch. 12.

5. Dickinson, "I dwell in Possibility" (466), in Franklin, ed., *Poems of Emily Dickinson*.

and not be a "waster" of them. Jesus said, "Do not let your hearts be troubled or afraid" (John 14:27). We are invited to deepen our trust in the Lord and to believe that somehow there is meaning and a reason for our sorrows.

There is a story of a prince and a beggar that exemplifies this point very well. Every day a very wealthy prince would ride in his ornate carriage through the countryside. Each day he would pass a poor beggar sitting along the side of the road. Whenever the prince saw the beggar, he would stop and walk over to the beggar. As he approached, the beggar would hold out his hand and the prince would give him several gold coins. Then they would both go on their way. One day, as they passed each other, the prince stopped and, as the beggar approached him, held out his hand to the beggar first. So the beggar reached into his little purse, took out a grain of corn, and placed it in the hand of the prince. Then they both went on their way. A little while later, the beggar stopped to rest along the side of the road. He opened his purse and discovered to his amazement that in place of the grain of corn that he had given to the prince, there was a piece of gold. Then the beggar began to cry because he wished that he had given all his pieces of corn to the prince!

So often in life, we are like the beggar trusting in the goodness of the prince—the Lord. We approach him with outstretched hands for so many things, and because of his love for us, he takes care of us. But sometimes, just like the prince, the Lord offers his hand to us first. It is then that we are invited to take something out of our bag of life and put it in the hand of the Lord. We are invited to trust him more deeply, that no matter what happens to us in life, he is there for us. We are invited to take our pieces of corn out of our bag because we believe that in some way he will turn each piece of corn into a piece of gold. It is that way with the mysteries and sorrows in our lives. It is that way with our unanswered questions. We take each of them out of our bag and place them into his hand, trusting that somehow he will transform them into something that is good for us.

Mystery requires that we relinquish an endless search for answers and "learn to love the questions themselves." It requires a willingness to not understand everything at times. Perhaps real wisdom lies in not seeking answers at all. After all these years, I have begun to wonder if the secret of living well is not in having all the answers but in pursuing unanswerable questions in the company of good friends.

Conclusion

THE WELL-KNOWN AUTHOR ABRAHAM Joshua Heschel reminded people that "just to be is a blessing. Just to live is holy." Although we certainly believe this, for most of us it is also easier to see the holiness in life wrapped up in a beautiful sunset compared to a dimension of life where sorrow prevails. And yet the challenge for each of us is not to be a "waster of sorrows" but, as Rilke says, to try and integrate our sorrows into our lives in a positive and healthy way.

Buried in every sorrow is the opportunity for growth. But often it takes time to discover what that growth truly is or how our sorrow can become holy. Everyone has sorrows in life. The crucial thing is what we do with them. We are all faced with a choice. We can either strive to integrate them into our lives in a positive and healthy way or we can crumble under the weight of our sorrows and feel overwhelmed. In the musical *Les Misérables*, Fantine sings about how her sorrows in life caused her dreams to die. Our challenge is to face into our sorrows so that the dreams we have about ourselves, the dreams about some part of our lives, the dreams about some dimension of our world, don't die. We don't want to let life kill the dreams we have dreamed.

George Bernanos ends his book *The Diary of a Country Priest* with the words, "Grace is everywhere." Maybe for each of us, the real challenge is to find grace in our sorrows. If we can do this, then not only will our sorrows become a blessing for us but we will also become a blessing to others. Then, not only will it help us individually, but we will also become the type of person who always tries "to take the pain out of things."

Ultimately, maybe our only refuge is in the goodness of each other.

Bibliography

Albom, Mitch. *Tuesdays with Morrie: An Old Man, A Young Man, and Life's Greatest Lesson.* New York: Doubleday, 1997.

Bernanos, George. *The Diary of a Country Priest.* New York: Doubleday, 1974.

Clapp, Rodney. "Eugene Peterson: A Monk Out of Habit," *Christianity Today,* April 1987, 23–26.

De Mello, Anthony. *The Heart of the Enlightened: A Book of Story Meditations.* New York: Doubleday, 1989.

Eliot, T. S. *The Complete Poems and Plays, 1909–1950.* New York: Harcourt, Brace, 1935.

Eckhart, Meister. *Breakthrough, Meister Eckhart's Creation Spirituality, in New Translation.* Introduction and commentaries by Matthew Fox. Garden City, NY: Image, 1980.

Franklin, R. W., editor. *The Poems of Emily Dickinson.* Cambridge, MA: Harvard University Press, 1999.

Freedman, Ralph. *Life of a Poet: Rainer Maria Rilke.* Evanston, IL: Northwestern University Press, 1998.

Goodall, Jane. *Reason for Hope: A Spiritual Journey.* New York: Warner, 1999.

Julian, of Norwich. *Showings.* Translated by Edmund Colledge and James Walsh. New York: Paulist, 1978.

Kelly, Thomas. *A Testament of Devotion.* New York: Harper, 1941.

King, Martin Luther, Jr. "Suffering and Faith." In *A Testament of Hope: The Essential Writings and Speeches of Martin Luther King, Jr,* edited by James Melvin Washington, 41–42. San Francisco: Harper & Row, 1986.

LeShan, Lawrence L. *How to Meditate: A Guide to Self-Discovery.* New York: Bantam, 1974.

Maslow, Abraham H. *The Psychology of Science: A Reconnaissance.* New York: Harper and Row, 1966.

Merton, Thomas. *The Wisdom of the Desert.* New York: New Directions, 1960.

Remen, Rachel Naomi. *My Grandfather's Blessings: Stories of Strength, Refuge, and Belonging.* New York: Riverhead, 2000.

Rilke, Rainer Maria. *Duino Elegies.* Translated by J. B. Leishman and Stephen Spender. New York: Norton, 1963.

————. *Letters to a Young Poet.* Translated by M. D. Herter. New York: Norton, 1934.

Saroyan, William. *The Human Comedy.* New York: Harcourt, Brace, 1943.

Smith, Barry M., and Betty Hamilton Pryce. *Reading for Power.* Providence, RI: Programs for Achievement in Reading, 1982.

Uhlein, Gabriele, and Hildegard, Saint. *Meditations with Hildegard of Bingen.* Santa Fe, NM: Bear and Co., 1983.

Untener, Ken. "Archbishop Oscar Romero Prayer: A Step Along the Way." Online: http://www.usccb.org/prayer-and-worship/prayers-and-devotions/prayers/archbishop_romero_prayer.cfm.

Weil, Simone. *First and Last Notebooks.* Translated by Richard Rees. New York: Oxford University Press, 1970.

Wiesel, Elie. *Night.* Translated by Stella Rodway. New York: Avon, 1960.

Zuck, Roy B. *The Speaker's Quote Book: Over 5,000 Illustrations and Quotations for All Occasions.* Grand Rapids: Kregel, 2009.

Made in the USA
Coppell, TX
01 May 2022

77269007R00039